With gratitude for the US military and their families—both those
who have served in the past and those who serve today

CS & DP

Text copyright © 2022 by Christina Soontornvat
Illustrations copyright © 2022 by Dow Phumiruk

First edition 2022

Library of Congress Catalog Card Number 2021953114
ISBN 978-1-5362-2205-0

22 23 24 25 26 27 CCP 10 9 8 7 6 5 4 3 2 1

Printed in Shenzhen, Guangdong, China

This book was typeset in Intro.
The illustrations were done in pencil and digital collage.

Candlewick Press
99 Dover Street
Somerville, Massachusetts 02144

www.candlewick.com

A LIFE OF SERVICE

The Story of Senator Tammy Duckworth

CHRISTINA SOONTORNVAT

illustrated by DOW PHUMIRUK

CANDLEWICK PRESS

Jj Kk Ll Mm Nn Oo Pp Qq Rr Ss Tt Uu Vv Ww Xx Yy Zz

Even before she ever touched American soil, Ladda Tammy Duckworth knew that she would someday serve her country.

Born in Bangkok, Thailand, Tammy is an American citizen who grew up traveling all over Southeast Asia with her family. Tammy's childhood was full of love and laughter: learning at school, joking with friends, going to Girl Scout meetings.

But Tammy knew that not all kids had such carefree lives.

Tammy's father worked for the United Nations, and his job meant that the family was never far from the echoes of war. When she was seven years old, Tammy sat on a rooftop watching bombs fall over Cambodia's capital city as her family waited to be evacuated. Tammy's father taught her how to trace the lights streaming across the sky so that she wouldn't be afraid.

One of Tammy's father's jobs was delivering aid to refugees who were fleeing violence in their home countries. When Tammy visited refugee camps with him, she met people who had lost almost everything. Many of the refugees hoped to start a new life in the United States. Even though the US had just lost a war in the region, for many people, America still represented freedom, democracy, and opportunity.

Tammy realized that her country's true power came not from its military might but from the ideals it had been founded upon. Filled with pride for a homeland she had yet to see, Tammy dreamed that one day she would be like the aid workers she met in the camps: serving America by helping those in need.

But before Tammy could go after her dream, her own family was struck by hardship. Her father lost his job, and the family used the last of their savings to move to Hawaii.

With her father out of work, they hovered on the edge of homelessness and relied on food stamps to buy groceries. On most days, the only food Tammy could count on was her school's reduced-price meals. Tammy's father would go without eating so that she would have the money to buy food at school; she would save her lunch and bring it home so that he could have something to eat.

At one point, Tammy was the only one in the family working. She sold flowers by the side of the road from a plastic bucket.

Even with all the pressures of keeping her family fed, Tammy was determined to soar at school. She played sports and ran on the track team. She studied during her lunch breaks and late into the night. By the time she graduated from high school, she was near the top of her class.

Finally, all of her relentless hard work had paid off. Her future was wide open. As she headed off to college and then to graduate school, Tammy still knew she wanted to serve her country. She just hadn't figured out the best way to do it yet.

Many of Tammy's classmates were veterans, and they encouraged Tammy to join the Reserve Officers' Training Corps.

When Tammy went to her first ROTC class, something clicked.

She loved the bonds of trust that she built with the other cadets. When there was a victory, it belonged to all of them. When things were tough, they were tough for everyone. When soldiers put on their uniforms, they were a unit, sworn to defend the Constitution and their country.

All that discipline and hard work she had put into school could now go toward something much bigger than herself. At last, here was a way to serve, and it felt right.

At the time, the only combat positions open to women were in aviation, and Tammy had her heart set on flying Black Hawk helicopters. In flight school, Tammy logged three extra hours in the flight simulator each night—more than any other student in her class. When she returned to her unit, she was promoted to first lieutenant and then became commander of Company B of the 106th Aviation unit of the Illinois Army National Guard.

Tammy fell in love with a soldier named Bryan Bowlsbey. They married and began building a new life together. She had led her unit for three years and was gliding toward a happy future when America declared war in Iraq.

TAMMY DUCKWORTH

30
31
38

BATTERY UTILITY
FIRST AID
AMMUNITION
46. COPILOT SIDE LOWER CONSOLE
47.AUXILIARY FUEL MANAGER PANEL

IGNITION LOCK
STOWAGE COMPART
STOWAGE BACK
STICK GRIP
IGNITION KEYLOCK
LOWER CONSOLE

45678910

35

49

50

Tammy disagreed with the US decision to invade Iraq, and her time as unit commander was up. Even so, she begged her battalion commander to let her stay with her company. If they were going into battle, she needed to be right there with them.

Her request was granted, and Tammy accompanied her unit to their base in Balad, Iraq. Tammy was a battle captain, planning and organizing helicopter missions. She lived for the days when she got to fly helicopters. She loved the feeling of speed and the power of sitting behind the controls of such a massive machine.

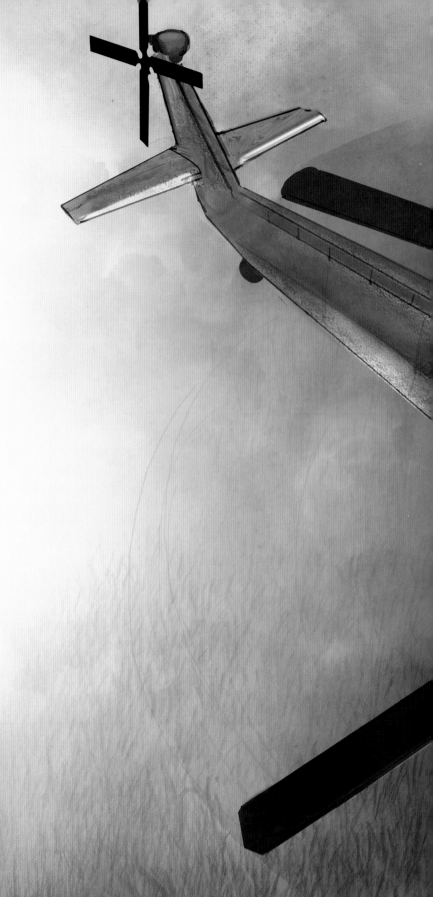

November 12, 2004, started out as a great day.

Tammy and her crew had been flying all day, picking up soldiers and delivering supplies.

They had just picked up their last passenger and were fifteen minutes from their base when Tammy heard the *tap-tap-tap* of gunfire.

Seconds later, a rocket-propelled grenade slammed into the helicopter.

A fireball burst through the aircraft. Black smoke filled the cockpit.

Tammy called out to her crew, but no one responded. She gripped the controls, trying to land. But her foot pedals wouldn't work. Something was wrong.

She had to land. She had to get her crew to safety.

And then everything went black.

Tammy's pilot-in-command, Chief Warrant Officer Dan Milberg, had been on the controls when they were hit, and he managed to land the aircraft. A second Black Hawk helicopter, not far behind, landed nearby to help rescue Tammy's crew.

Dan and the other soldiers hurried to drag the injured out of the smoking wreckage. When Dan saw Tammy, he was sure she was dead. But even under threat of enemy fire, he would not leave her body behind.

Sergeant Chris Fierce lay beside Tammy in the rescue helicopter as it sped back to base. He had been severely wounded, and they needed to get him treated fast.

Chris looked at Tammy's body and noticed something— a faint, fluttering sign of life. Could it be possible that she had survived?

Chris was in tremendous pain, but when they landed, he shouted to the medics that they must treat Tammy first.

Tammy received the critical care she needed to live. But when she woke, her life would never be the same.

The grenade blast had destroyed both of her legs. It nearly destroyed her right arm.

When she first arrived at the hospital, Tammy's body rejected the pain medications the doctors gave her, and the agony of her injuries was overwhelming. She lived in a dark cloud of unending pain that rolled over her body again and again.

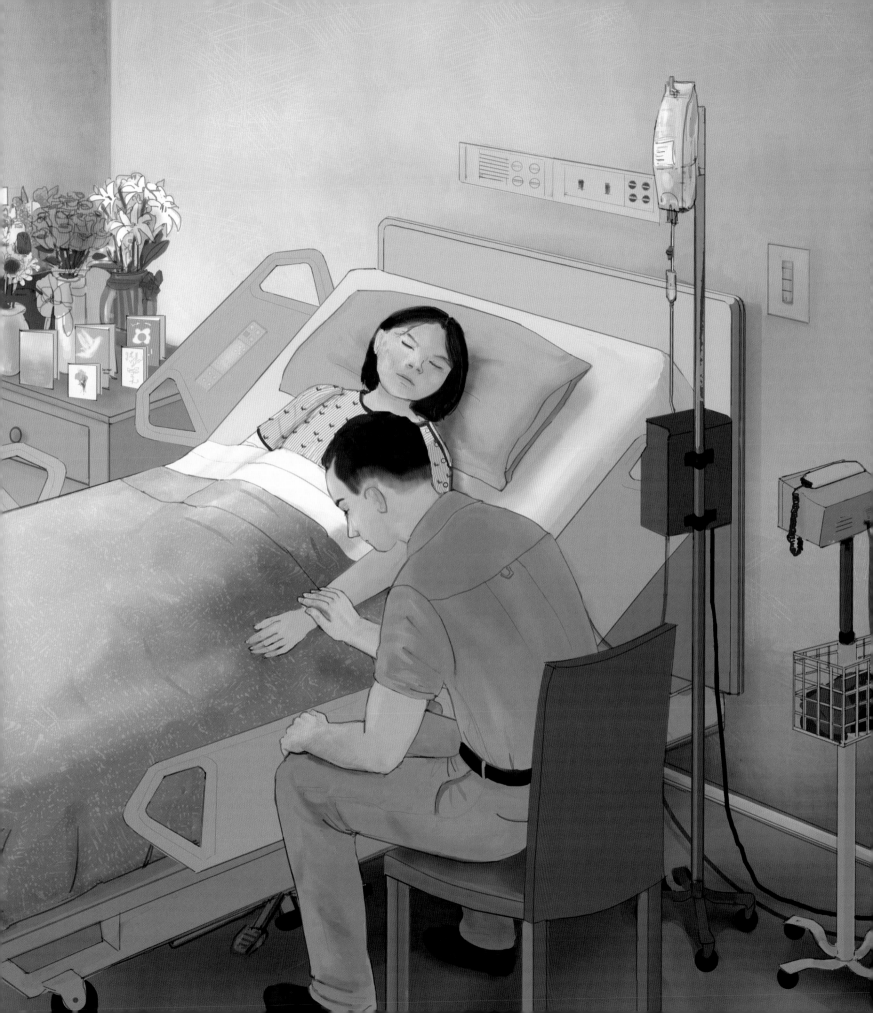

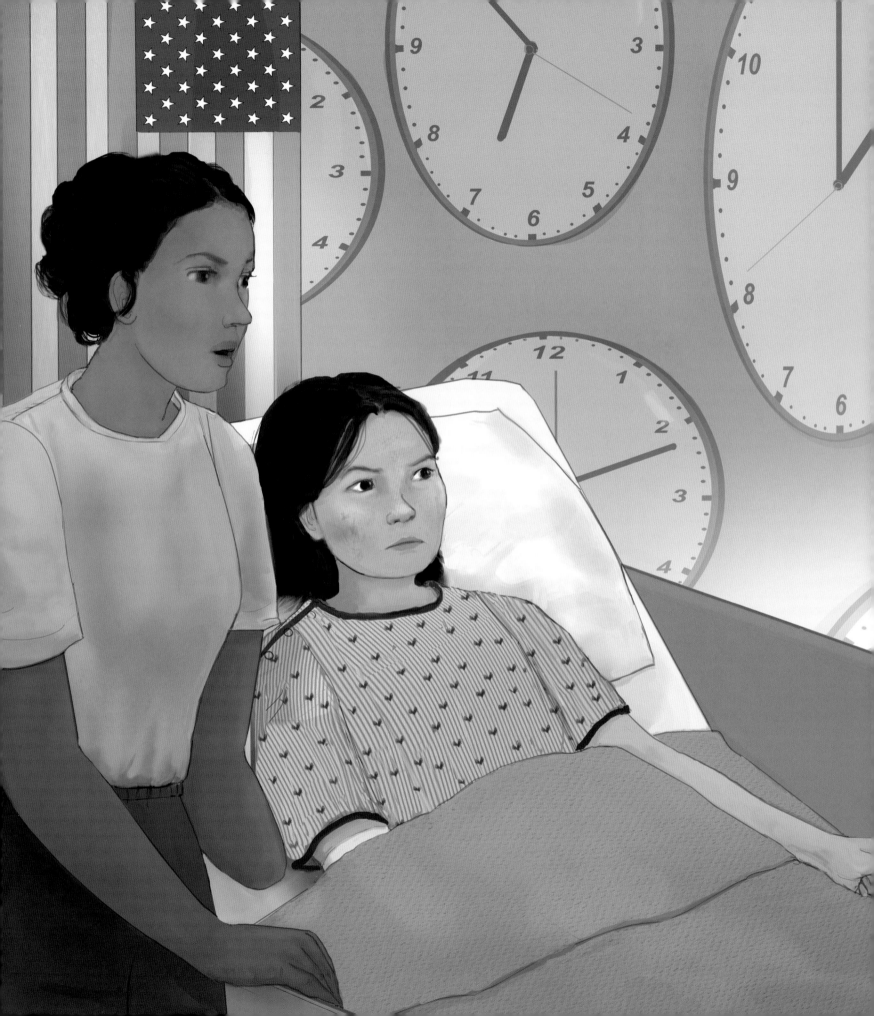

Sergeant First Class Juanita Wilson, a recovering arm amputee at the hospital, came to Tammy's room. Juanita understood how bad the pain was, and she knew that Tammy could make it out the other side. Together, the women used the clock on the wall to count through the seconds. When they got to 60, they began again.

For five days, Juanita stood at Tammy's bedside, helping her live through one minute at a time, one hour at a time, and then one more.

Once the pain became more bearable, Tammy had to relearn how to eat. How to bathe. It took all her strength just to sit up. After months of treatment, she was determined to learn to walk again.

The doctors fit Tammy with prosthetic legs. Her right leg was gone all the way to the hip, and controlling her new prosthetic was like balancing on the end of a broomstick.

Each day was a battle against gravity.

Inch by inch, falling, getting up, and falling again.

And again.

Get back up.

Keep fighting.

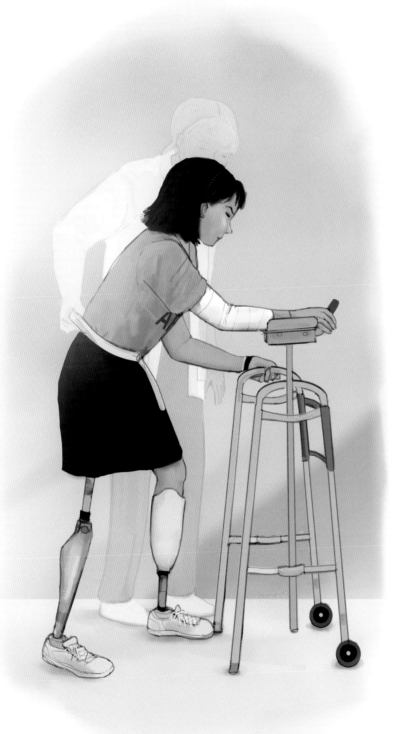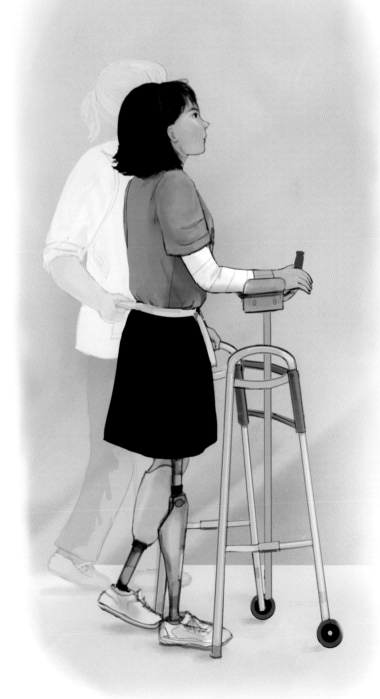

Tammy battled through her recovery, strengthening her right arm and learning how to use her new prosthetic legs. Her ultimate goal was to get in shape so she could return to combat. But life had a different trajectory in store.

Tammy was the highest-ranking amputee in the hospital, so other soldiers often came to her, asking for help getting the healthcare they needed. Tammy kept busy making calls to elected officials on their behalf, demanding the US give veterans the respect and treatment they deserved.

Then one day she got a call of her own.

A senator from her home state of Illinois urged Tammy to consider serving in a different way: by running for the US House of Representatives. He told her that Congress could use more leaders with military service who understood the realities and risks of war.

This was a big decision. It would mean that Tammy might never return to fight alongside her fellow soldiers. But maybe this was a way that she could still fight for her country.

The day after she checked out of the hospital, Tammy announced that she would run for the US House of Representatives.

She was grateful for all the work she had put into getting her body battle-ready, because the campaign was relentless. She had searing phantom pains on the bottom of her missing feet, but she had to walk, stand, and talk, hour after hour, day after day.

As hard as she worked, she still lost that race.

But by then, Tammy knew how much the people of Illinois needed her. There were too many families without healthcare. Too many people living in poverty. She couldn't give up on them.

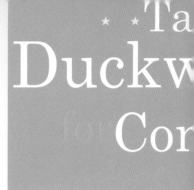

She decided to try again, and this time she won her House race.

A few years later, Tammy decided to run for the Senate. Her opponent in that race mocked her when she stated that her ancestors had served in the military going all the way back to the American Revolution. To him, it was impossible that someone with Tammy's Thai heritage could also descend from a long line of American heroes. Tammy's response to his racism was to defeat him soundly. She would not let someone else's ignorance hold her back.

The Daily News
Illinois
November 8, 2016

FIRST THAI AMERICAN WOMAN TO SERVE IN CONGRESS

First Female Amputee to Serve in Congress

When Tammy was sworn in as senator, she racked up a long string of firsts.

November 9, 2016

CONGRATULATIONS SENATOR DUCKWORTH

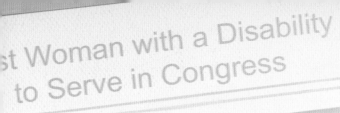
st Woman with a Disability
to Serve in Congress

National Newsline
First Senator to Give
Birth While in Office

The birth of her second daughter brought another milestone. In 2018, Tammy pushed the US Senate to change the chamber rules to allow her to bring her ten-day-old baby onto the floor so that Tammy could cast her vote.

Senator Duckworth continues to break barriers and defy expectations. Her crew risked their lives to give her a second chance. She doesn't plan on wasting one single moment.

As a proud veteran, Tammy has spoken out against rushing to war. She has pushed for the US to do more to help refugees. She has fought for equal rights for women and transgender people in the military. She has worked to protect the rights of people with disabilities. And Tammy has never stopped fighting for the care and dignity of America's veterans. Throughout her career, she has put her body, her voice, and her heart into service of her country.

Service has given Tammy the chance to soar.

She wants everyone to have that chance.

Together, there is more work to do.

Tammy's country still needs her.

And she plans to keep fighting.

TIME LINE OF MAJOR LIFE EVENTS

March 12, 1968: Ladda Tammy Duckworth is born in Bangkok, Thailand, to Lamai Sompornpairin and US Marine Captain Franklin G. Duckworth.

1976: Tammy learns to speak English. She remains fluent in Thai and Indonesian as her family moves around Southeast Asia following her father's aid work.

1984: Tammy's family moves to Hawaii.

1985: Graduates from McKinley High School in Honolulu

1989: Graduates from the University of Hawaii with a degree in political science

1990: Joins ROTC while attending George Washington University, where she earns her master's degree in international affairs in 1992

1992: Commissioned as a second lieutenant in the Army Reserve

1993: Attends flight school at Fort Rucker, Alabama

1993: Marries Major Bryan Bowlsbey

1996: Joins the Illinois Army National Guard while pursuing a PhD in political science at Northern Illinois University. In 1998, she is promoted to captain.

2004: Tammy's unit begins their deployment in Balad, Iraq. On November 12, 2004, her helicopter is shot down by insurgents.

2005: Spends thirteen months in recovery and rehabilitation at Walter Reed Army Medical Center

2006: Unsuccessfully runs for a US House seat

2006: Named director of the Illinois Department of Veterans Affairs

2009: Sworn in as assistant secretary for public and intergovernmental affairs for the US Department of Veterans Affairs

2010: Earns her fixed-wing pilot's license

2012: Elected to the US House of Representatives

2014: Re-elected to her House seat. Retires from military service as a lieutenant colonel in the Illinois Army National Guard

2014: Gives birth to daughter Abigail Okalani Bowlsbey

2016: Elected to the US Senate

2018: Becomes the first US senator to give birth while in office, to daughter Maile Pearl Bowlsbey

TAMMY DUCKWORTH'S ONGOING LEGACY OF SERVICE

IMMIGRATION AND REFUGEES

Tammy Duckworth has urged the Senate to protect family-sponsored immigration (2013) and called on Congress to accept refugees, regardless of their nationality, race, or religion (2020). In 2019, she introduced legislation to provide benefits to immigrant veterans and protect their families from deportation.

POVERTY, EDUCATION, AND SOCIAL WELFARE

Senator Duckworth has defended the SNAP program, which helps low-income and no-income Americans purchase food (2017), and introduced the Military Hunger Prevention Act (2018). She introduced legislation to improve public housing and make it accessible to those with disabilities (2019) and sponsored legislation to help all students gain access to higher education and high-paying jobs (2019).

MILITARY AND VETERANS

Duckworth introduced the Troop Talent Act to help returning veterans find work (2013) and cosponsored the Clay Hunt Suicide Prevention for American Veterans Act (2015). She advocated for lifting the ban on women serving in military combat (2012) and opposed the ban against transgender personnel in the military (2019). She serves on the Senate Armed Services Committee.

DISABILITY RIGHTS

Senator Duckworth fought to protect the Americans with Disabilities Act (2018) and cosponsored legislation to help those with prosthetics be covered under insurance (2020). In 2020, she received an ADA Legacy Award from the American Association of People with Disabilities for her advocacy for disability rights.

FAMILIES

Duckworth introduced the Friendly Airports for Mothers Improvement Act (2015) and the Fairness for Breastfeeding Mothers Act (2019). She cosponsored a House bill to increase access to maternity care (2016) and has introduced legislation to make workplaces more family-friendly, increase access to childcare, and help low-income families obtain diapers (2019). In 2018, she introduced the 21st Century American Service Act to ensure that every American civilian has a fulfilling opportunity to serve their country.

THE ENVIRONMENT

Senator Duckworth serves on the Senate Committee on Environment and Public Works and cofounded the Senate Environmental Justice Caucus. She sponsored the Great Lakes Water Protection Act (2019) and served on the Senate Democrats' Special Committee on the Climate Crisis (2019–2020).

"That day, I lost both of my legs, but I was given a second chance at life. It's a feeling that has helped to drive me in my second chance at service—no one should be left behind, and every American deserves another chance."

LEARN MORE ABOUT TAMMY DUCKWORTH

CBS This Morning. "Note to Self: Sen. Tammy Duckworth." April 12, 2018. https://youtu.be/P_Q1luJAqSw.

Girl Scouts of the U.S.A. "Storytellers: Major Tammy Duckworth." May 30, 2013. https://youtu.be/KOSyqxbyxLo.

Howell, Janet, and Theresa Howell. *Leading the Way: Women in Power.* Somerville, MA: Candlewick Press, 2019.

Jopp, Kelsey. *Tammy Duckworth.* Groundbreaking Women in Politics. Lake Elmo, MN: Focus Readers, 2020.